Nightjar

Books by Michael Simms

POEMS
Nightjar
American Ash
Migration

CHAPBOOKS
Black Stone
The Happiness of Animals
The Fire-eater
Notes on Continuing Light

TEXTBOOKS WITH JACK MYERS
Dictionary of Poetic Terms
Longman Dictionary and Handbook of Poetry

Nightjar

Michael Simms

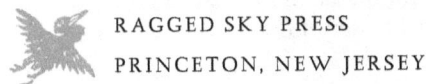
RAGGED SKY PRESS
PRINCETON, NEW JERSEY

Published by Ragged Sky Press
270 Griggs Drive, Princeton, NJ 08540
www.raggedsky.com

Library of Congress Control Number: 2021944834
ISBN: 978-1-933974-43-9

Book design: Jean Foos

Cover design: Dirk Rowntree

Cover art: John James Audubon, *Chuck-will's-Widow*, (also known as Nightjar), from *Birds of America*, published 1827–1838.

Photograph of author: Eva-Maria Simms

This book has been composed in FF Scala and LTC Kaatskill
Printed in the United States of America
First Edition

For Janie Lu Cook Simms
(1933–2012)

Leave the front door open.
Leave the back door open.
Let the ghosts enter.
Let the ghosts leave.

—M. S.

Contents

IV.

I.

Coming to Terms

I remember standing at the window
watching the snow fall slowly
through the afternoon.
It was one of those April snows
we used to get in Pittsburgh
before America went to hell.

I'd just returned from spilling
my parents' ashes in the Llano River
behind their house, probably
an act of *thanagogic* vandalism
of a municipal water supply
but who's to know?

And watching the snowflakes
melt as fast as they hit the sidewalk,
I felt a bit *ghostalgic*, a word
I may have invented
for that occasion to mark
a feeling of nostalgia

for another world, the one
we came from and will return to,
and also the feeling of affection
for the dead, at least for
my mother, a kind and wise
woman who subtly saved me

from my father, a cruel vain man
whom I've come to accept
genuinely despised me.
But I didn't hate or dislike him
instead I *disloved* him, feeling
an intense disappointment

at his limitations, opportunities
for love being so few in this life.

And as each snowflake fell
on the sidewalk immediately
disappearing as if meant
to live only in the air, of the air,

I was feeling *astralgic*, a sadness
for the stars that died
billions of years ago
whose light we see now,
a homesickness for a cosmos
that no longer exists.

There is no lasting happiness
in this world, only
particles of happiness,
fleeting, unpredictable,
transitory as a fragrance
or a falling leaf or a glance

from a passerby on the street,
a plain person, hardly noticeable
who slips through our dreams
like a cat through shadows
changing us in ways
we never wanted to be changed.

Petrichor

What we smell after a rain
is called *petrichor*
from *petra*, rock

and *ichor*, the fluid flowing
like blood in the veins
of the Greek gods—and

the water discharged from
a wound. *Petrichor*,
a recent coinage, first appeared

in a 1964 paper by
two Australian chemists
to signify the smell

previously known as
argillaceous odor.
Clearly a better word was needed.

Being on the spectrum
of weirdness, I'm remembering all this
from a dictionary I wrote

decades ago, etymologies
staying with me like pieces
of interesting trash stuck

to the bottom of my shoe.
It is evening. The rain has stopped
and my dog is dragging me

through the neighborhood
and ichor is flowing
all around us, dripping

from the oaks and maples, weighing
down the hostas, glistening
in the spaces between azalea

petals, as if I had forever
to spend in this reverie
of words in the evening

of my life, but I smell curry
and my stomach is *wambling*
and hunger goes right down

to my tiniest toes and fingers
which, by the way, are called *minimi*.
Did you know the first cry of a newborn

is called a *vagitus*?
And the diffused glow you see
through your closed eyes

is called *phosphene*? It's possible
to drift through life entirely
unaware

the space between your eyebrows
is the *glabella*
and the space between your nostrils

is the *columella nasi*, but why
live in the gap
between words? Knowing

the name of a thing lets you
sing. A teenager walks by
earbud chanting

hey girl hey girl hey girl
stick stick make it move
stick stick make it move

which leads me to conclude
not every *vocable* is a poem—
or maybe it is, just as

every joke begs to be taken seriously
because life itself is
an *interrobang*—

an unanswerable question shouted
in the face of the growing
dark.

Meconium

A few days after my daughter was born
she passed the last stool
of meconium,

a viscous dark tar,
olive-green, shaped like a flower,
odorless, composed

of what she digested
in the womb: epithelial cells
of her own intestine, lanugo,

mucus, bile and of course
amniotic fluid,
the womb-water where she floated

dreaming of God.
Wiping her, I felt at first disgusted,
as if I were cleaning up

after my dog
but then I remembered this
is my daughter and this

dark tar is her mother's
womb still clinging
so

it is sacred, the way
soil clinging to the seed
of a new shoot

pushing out of the earth
is sacred, the seed
somehow understanding

its joyful task.
My new daughter laughed
for the first time

at the small
pleasure of passing waste
made pure

by the loving hands
of a man who suddenly thinks
Holy Shit

Satan and the Snowman

Many Christmases ago
I was in a toy store shopping
for my daughter when I saw

a man in his twenties, a store
employee, leaning toward
a shelf of snowmen dressed

in little top hats and plaid
scarves, and the young man said
quite distinctly HAIL SATAN

and all the snowmen repeated
HAIL SATAN. Startled I stepped
back, knocking over a display case

of Bikini Barbies. Then I saw a sign
above the young man's head,
Mimicking Snowmen. Holy

Jesus I thought, what
has Christmas come to?
What have I come to,

trapped between
demonic Frosties
and anorexic Barbies?

       *

When I was eight I was raped
by an older boy. It wasn't
brutal, more seduction

than assault, but I bled
for days. As I grew up,
I remembered it rarely, as if

it was just one of those things
boys do. Maybe it was.
How would I know,

having led only one life?
But I know this: when
a boy buries a secret

he grows to be a man
who hurts others. It's simple:
A heart that's broken

breaks hearts. So I followed
a daisy chain of secret betrayals,
small thefts, rehearsed summaries

of the faults of my lovers,
perfectly timed accusations
and insincere reconciliations.

      *

I don't have relationships,
the old drunk explained
with surprising wisdom,

I take hostages.
To stay married
a man must forgive

his wife for loving him.
But why buy the cow
when manure is free? I think.

You can, as I did for many years,
drift from love to love as if
betrayal were the answer to longing.

      *

A man feeling unworthy of love
can't enter his own house
so he stands in the front yard

hoping to gain the courage
to join his family. It is winter.
Snow is falling. Through

the front window he sees
the brightly decorated tree,
his wife and children

in front of the fireplace
and yet he can't bring himself
to enter the warmth.

He finds if he stands still
and lets the snow fall on him,
he feels somewhat warmer.

He takes off his clothes and lets
his skin freeze. At last he's warm.
The snow falls steadily covering

his head and shoulders,
arms and hands. His feet
lock in ice. His eyes, ears, nose

cake with snow. His joints stiffen.
His arms become crooked branches,
his eyes lumps of coal, his nose

a ridiculous carrot. He breathes snow
until his lungs are full. He eats snow
until his guts are solid with the stuff.

His daughter comes out of the house
kindly wraps a plaid scarf
around his neck, balances a top hat

on the snowball of his head.
How are you, Daddy? she asks
I'm fine he says. And he is. He's fine.

The Dark

Beauty didn't interest me.
Bats did. I was
a budding nerd

who'd already memorized
everything I could find about
the 17 species of bats

nesting in Carlsbad Caverns
and now my imagination was aroused
by the possibility of seeing the nursery

of the Brazilian free-tailed
where a colony of millions
hung upside down

nourishing their babies with
milk, not insects, as I explained
to my mother who gleamed with pride

at her little chiropterologist.
The bats flew out of the cave
in a huge black cloud every evening

to hunt insects and haunt
the countryside, returning at dawn
using *echolocation*, I explained

to my mother. The nursery
was off-limits to families on the tour of course
but I had plans of sneaking away.

                    *

The park ranger herded us down
the chained path sloping into the earth
until we came to a cathedral

where columns of rock caught the light
and shimmered. If beauty
had been my thing this was it

but it wasn't. I was impatient
to see the flutter-mice I'd come for
and nothing less. In a sonorous voice

the ranger said to us, his congregation,
Absolute darkness is rare.
Even if you lock yourself in a closet

at night during a blackout
a small amount of light
will seep into your eyes.

He said he would turn off the lights
for 30 seconds. *Just 30 seconds,*
he said, *but it will feel like*

a lifetime. Then the world, everything
I knew went dark and I gasped
for light

as if it were air and breathed in
nothing I knew. Confusion,
panic, calm, exhilaration

washed over me. I breathed
the darkness into my lungs,
felt the darkness on my skin

not an absence but a texture
which now, half a century later,
I might name

the black fabric of my unconscious
although at the age of 11
all I knew was a rising panic

that dissolved
into pure
imperishable awe.

       *

In that darkness
the chronic angers of my family
which had ruled my life

receded, as did school
which bored me, my supposed
friends whom I suspected

pitied me, and the whole
shoddy apparatus of my life
as an autistic kid

who hadn't learned to speak
until he was five,
an easy target for bullies and abusers,

a kid who had climbed into himself
and found so little in the empty attic
of a soul full of broken toys,

he'd accepted
his role as the loneliest boy
on the planet, a perpetual

party of one, a specter
on the spectrum. Having been
silent almost half my life

I hadn't gotten the hang
of being pleasant, so I relied
on the illusion of intelligence—

a tiresome authority on insects,
a memorizer of maps and tables,
a secret lover of Dean Martin,

a singer of the music
of scientific names—
this life, the only one

I would know for decades—
faded away in the dark
like a bad dream I could wake from

simply by turning out the lights
and the darkness inside me
would merge with

the darkness of the world
and I would feel whole
and, if not happy,

at least at peace with
this sorry lot I'd been given
through no fault

of my own. The world
of darkness would be mine
and, like a comic book hero

who'd fought the demons
and won, I would have
my own kingdom and with

a gentle hand I'd rule
the gentle dead
who'd welcome me home.

                    *
And when the lights came back on
and the cavern beckoned
with its precarious

paths, low
ceilings and huge opera halls,
stadiums of jeweled earth

and the slight breeze coming
from even deeper
darknesses

below, nothing in the tour
of those magnificent caves
and their tight squeezes that led to hippodromes

and amphitheaters crowded with stone spectators
who'd witnessed the slow accumulation
of calcium ghosts

in the galleries of ancient coral beds,
not the Hall of Giants
or the Crystal Spring Dome,

not the stone elephants
or the fine filigree of red minerals,
or the stone draperies

and lily pads suspended from the ceiling,
or the cave pearls, the gypsum flowers,
the chandelier ballroom of massive speleothems,

or the water dripping from the ceiling for eons
shaping the great cities uninhabited by the living,
or the tempting mysteries of Lake Lebarge

with its blind white fish who'd never seen daylight,
nor even the 138 miles of the forbidden wilderness
of the Lechuguilla Cave

awakened my innocence
and longing
as this song, this

beckoning
from the underbelly of the world
this darkness singing

come home, come home
little one
we've been waiting for you.

      *

As we passed the sign
showing the way
to the *bat nursery,* which

was the ranger's cue
for a scripted joke about Batman,
I ducked

out of line and moved toward
the narrow passage, but
my mother gently

reined me in
and I stayed with her
through the tour, discovering

a group of sleeping bats is called
a *cauldron*
and in flight, a *cloud*

and that evening
we returned to watch from the amphitheater
the black cloud of bats leaving the rocky entrance

and gaining speed like wind-blown smoke
sweeping over the Chihuahuan Desert
with a horizontal speed of up to 100 mph,

each soul catching and eating up to half of
its half-ounce weight
in flies, crickets, maggots,

and I envied their nimble flight
on quick fierce wings
and I wanted to return

not to the cave, but to
the darkness, those 30 seconds
flying through

the stone passageways
navigating by sound and
instinct

out of the cave and up
to the reddening sky, the slender moon
bright as a sword.

                *

Yes, I knew I would return
to this nothingness, this absence
where I could blossom

like a stone flower,
a stalactite
growing slowly, invisibly

in the darkness that rose
like a slight breeze
from the chambers below

where even
my own breath seemed
unbearably loud,

this quick fierce movement
like wings at the beginning of my feeling
life, this moment when the past

and future melded
and time
no longer flowed

like water
but flowed like rock
and even now, here

in this darkness I still contain,
I feel completely and blessedly empty
and my own death begins to sing.

Dandelion

I wonder whether
my neighbor knows
what he's doing,

spraying poison
on the dandelions
in his yard. The taproots

push down twelve feet,
drawing nutrients
to the surface, enriching

the soil. The grass
of his lawn will grow
lush on the gift

of nutrients until
Taraxacum officinale
can't compete with

taller, faster,
shallow-rooted grasses
running across the surface

of the dirt. In a year or two
the dandelion disappears
from the yard, having already

thrown its seed to the wind.
I wonder whether
my neighbor has noticed

the yellow flowers opening at dawn
and closing at dusk
like us or

the broken stems exuding
a milky latex that tastes
of regret or

the florets arranging themselves
into blowballs
of fine barbed hairs.

I want to tell my neighbor,
my friend who's kind to my dog
and courteous to my wife,

who waves at me now
as he carries groceries
from his car,

the *dents-de-lion* is edible
from white root to yellow flowerhead,
its tender medicine

exactly what our polluted bodies
need, its abundant florets
a vital spring nectar

for the bees. The science nerd
in me wants to say
the tap-rooted, perennial,

herbaceous dandelion
quickly adapts to local stressors
resulting in thousands of

microspecies, but in the end
I smile and wave at my neighbor
who, like me

and the Norwegian rat,
the smallpox virus,
and the tree of heaven

belongs to an invasive species
nature will deal with
in due time. I want to explain

we should be more
like this weed, inconspicuous
in the cracks of sidewalk,

tenacious, useful,
with deep roots and a sly
life, resourceful, finding our home

in the disturbed earth,
leaving the tired soil better
than we found it. The winged

seed clings to our clothes,
lifts on the wind from passing trains,
spreading with us across

the continent
while we unknowingly carry
the corrective to our sins.

In the cracks of asphalt,
in the broken ground,
in the abandoned field

of the demolished house,
among the tumble of brick
and block and rebar rising out of rubble,

out of bomb crater and bulldozed gravel,
out of disaster and mayhem,
out of ugly order and disorder,

out of beautiful neglect
wilding occurs, and so
on thin white wings

the seed settles
unnoticed,
bringing life to ruined places.

Nigel

I've been reading an obituary
About Nigel
The lonely gannet of Mana Island
Who fell in love
With a concrete statue

And I've been wondering
What his story says
About desire
Because I've come to believe
Without desire there is nothing

   *

Nigel with no other gannets
On the island
Wooed a fake bird
Building her
A nest of dirt and seaweed

Like Nigel we exist
Only because desire urges us
Toward the world

You might say
The beloved
Is the world and the reason
For the world

We are desire
Nothing but desire
You might say

   *

Conservationists hoped
The colony
Of 80 fake birds
Would attract real birds
And establish a breeding colony

But Nigel was the only gannet
Who arrived and he stayed
For her

It's important to know
That without the reaching
There is nothing
Without desire we do not exist

No matter if the beloved
Is a fantasy no matter
Whether memories
Are real

*

Nigel was a lovely bird
One woman said
But a bit confused
He was likely kicked out
Of another colony and so
He came here

The real and the ideal
Live side by side
On the island

Noesis and *noema*
Hold hands
Or in this case
Wings

*

We want to believe
Nigel was happy
Living alone
With her

And then
Three gannets arrived
And built nests

But Nigel shunned the new arrivals
And remained on the other side
Of the island
With her

Like many of us
He preferred the ideal
To the real

      *

We love. We hate
We accept. We reject
We exist only because we desire

Last week Nigel's body was found
Next to his concrete love
By ranger Chris Bell
Who also lives alone on the island

Unknown Couple (charcoal/paper/watercolor)

He first noticed them because
        their backs were to the sea
sitting on the bench facing
        the people walking by

He sketched
        the arch of a shoulder
the movement of a hand
        the woman's head

turned and tilted slightly
        toward the man who
looks toward the mountains
        behind the artist

Both man and woman are bundled
        in heavy coats, a magnificent
sunset behind them but they've seen
        all this before

the artist thinks maybe
        they've grown bored
with gaudy sunsets and now
        are watching

the more subtle beauty of the land
        rising toward the blue
mountains and beyond. The woman
        wears a woolen

head scarf, the man
        a fisherman's cap, but
he doesn't have the hands
        of a fisherman

the artist thinks, more the hands of
        say an accountant

or teacher, soft yet certain, yes
    a couple of retired

teachers the artist presumes. The woman
    clutches the scarf
tightly against the wind, a light
    spray of the sea

against jagged rocks, birds circling
    over the reddening
water behind her. The artist
    somehow knows

the couple is the center of
    the story, the other
people walking by or standing
    at the rail looking out

at the corrasions of weather are merely
    suggestions, local
color in a colorless city
    estranged from

his attention, the eye
    so subtle compared
to a possible sketch, he must make
    each line a gesture

of the moment, refined, distilled
    twisting in place
as the wind blows across the paper
    lifting the birds

on extended wings which then fold
    into dives below the paper's
surface. A plastic cup blown by the wind
    catches on a rock and

he captures the distraction
    with a single gesture

of the charcoal. The couple
    looks settled into

place, belonging by
    long habit, the man
with deep lines on his face,
    the woman perhaps

younger, squints at him, not gazing,
    just a quick
read of his mood. The artist moves
    his hand to their shoes

the man's brogans as they used
    to call these thick-soled
lace-ups, scratched and scuffed,
    still serviceable, but her

shoes are delicately tooled leather
    not new
carefully polished
    a design of red and black

Spanish perhaps, elegant
    and expensive, her gloves
red and black as well perhaps
    bought at the same

shop they discovered in Madrid
    the artist imagines
their tenderness when
    alone, an old couple

in love. The old man's hands
    burrow
into the pockets of his great coat
    his affections

disguised, known only
    to the woman

who holds his arm in fierce
        possession which

he doesn't seem to mind
        at all, comfortable
in the habitual grip of the very
        married. Later

the artist washes the scene
        in watercolor, a blur
of rust and blue-gray
        over the drawing

of the old couple's
        practiced comfort together
solving the formal challenge
        of the layers of tension

between the subtle intimacy of
        the couple almost invisible
among strangers and the crashing waves
        spraying spumes into the air
and the wine-blue sea darkening

Only You

I woke this morning remembering the room we had in Paris which looked out on the Seine.

But we've never been to Paris.

Oh, of course we have. We took long walks along the river, and there was that old man with thousands of used books lined up on tables, and you found me a copy of James Wright's *Beautiful Ohio*.

Do you mean the poem? "Beautiful Ohio" is a poem, not a book.

Actually, "Beautiful Ohio" is a river. Perhaps I'm thinking of the time years ago when we had a room in Martins Ferry that looked out on the river, the beautiful Ohio River, and we took long walks in the crisp air. The maples were in their autumn glory, I remember.

Yes, you picked up a leaf from the ground, and on the back of the leaf you wrote a poem to me, something about leaves. There was also a dog in the poem. There's always a dog in your poems.

You're thinking of the Youghiogheny River. And it wasn't you, it was someone else.

You walked along the Youghiogheny River with someone else?

Oh, no, it was you, always you, but you may have been someone else at the time. Someone who looked like you and wrote your poems.

Well, at least we'll always have Paris. And the poems we wrote there.

Yes, we'll always have Paris where Ella sang so beautifully about the springtime, and we'll have other cities and other rivers where we've never been. And you and I will always sit on the grassy slope of the cemetery above Martins Ferry, Ohio, and look down at the valley and the bridge to West Virginia where the mountains are steep and beautiful, and we'll always love Appalachia in autumn.

That wasn't me. You must have done those things with someone else.

No, it was you. It was always you. Only you.

The Door

The first time I saw him
he was a beautiful Irish boy,
an extra in a Synge play

wearing too much
rouge on his cheeks which
might have looked clownish

on anyone less attractive.
Black curls, blue eyes,
delicate flesh bulging

in his forearms, his beauty
caught my breath as if
I'd swallowed a large

piece of meat. He
was radiant and this was
the first time I'd ever noticed

male beauty. I was 18,
a Southern Baptist boy.
Later he and I had

a poetry workshop together
and his similes were
as lush as his lips.

I could barely speak but
I knew he knew
I was attracted to him so

one day he invited me
to his apartment on the pretext
of loaning me a book

and all I could do
was nod silently. We both
knew the agenda. We sat

on the couch side by side
and he produced
a balm which

he rubbed slowly on his lips
to make them more
sensitive he said and

offered the balm
to me. My lips
began to tingle

as he moved his face
closer to mine and
in that moment I needed

to decide. If I made love
with him, it would be my first
time with a man.

It was Texas.
1972. Sodomy
was a felony. Also

I had a kind and pretty
girlfriend whom
I didn't want to hurt.

But now five decades later
I must be honest
at least with myself

if not you, reader who
may also have denied
denied, denied.

The truth is
my fear of jail and infidelity
paled next

to my fear of what
came next. You might say
I feared becoming

what I feared. I knew
if I made love with
this beautiful young man

I would fall in love
and then what?
I'd been taught

for a man to lie with a man
was abomination.
Although I didn't believe it,

had teachers who were gay,
I was worried
I would like sex with him

too much, need more, become
something my family
abhorred. Would he and I

bathe together, would we
take turns? What exactly
did his belly

feel like? I was curious,
ravenous, burning
with the lust

of the men of Sodom
who tried to rape
the visiting

angel. A taste
for strange flesh brought
the city to ruin. And yet

this young man's beauty
hypnotized me so I
sat on the couch unable to move

toward or away
from his lips, unable
to decide who I was,

what my life would be
but finally
didn't have to. He sensed

my fear and pulled back.
He was no seducer.
He didn't have to be, as

gorgeous as he was.
He sat back.
We made small talk.

I walked out the door.
For the rest of the semester
we saw each other often

but our eyes never met.
Why would they?
What was there to discuss?

A faltering glimpse of desire?
An interlude of uncertainty?
A door forever closed.

I Grow Old (Everything is disappearing)

I don't even remember my friend's name
But I will die calling his lover Eleanor
Because it was the name of the street
Where I saw her returning one afternoon
From the university, both of us knowing
He'd died the night before

In those days I was a scarecrow
And she was a pale young woman
I never had more than simple words
With her, always courteous
We once discussed swallows
I believe, nothing more

Four Meditations on the Ghostly Body of Estrangement

Moving the Piano

Levers wheels
ropes pulleys
simple machines the universe

gives us
to haul the music
up the melody
of stairs

but we slipped
and the piano went bumping
down the steps
playing
a John Cage tune

that night I dreamed
a whole symphony
of pianos thrown from windows
dropping from the backs of trucks
sliding down brick streets

car horns
cursing cabbies
police sirens

joining the frenzy
of chaotic
song

An Old Man's Feet

The brave arches
    have sprung the body forward
ten million times

the smell, ah the smell

of an old man's feet
like the smell of the earth
    after a rain

and the littlest toes
    like twins
poorest of poor relations

    Brother

every summer
starlings commit suicide
against the glass

crows fly over golden fields
in love with their shadows
a scarecrow flaps an empty arm
in the wind

Brother, I'm sorry I hurt you
wherever you are
please come home

we can begin again

    Dear Covid

You made us wise
for a while

well-acquainted with sorrow

but as we enter
our new lives

will we remember

the faster we moved
the sicker we got

Compost

I slide back the lid
of the compost bin
and a cloud of flies

rises with the raw
stench and I see
creatures thriving

in the dark—nematodes,
snails, slugs, wrigglers
seething in the riot

of banana skins, rotifera
twisting through
apple cores releasing

sweetness, feather-winged
beetles digesting
leftover minestrone

and hard crusts
of bread softening
and turning black
with time

        Sowbugs
and the bugs
that feed on them,

rove beetles, predatory
mites, formicid ants
and carabid—

We should be grateful
to them all, especially
the invisible mesophilic

bacteria who do
the principled work
of death

In the busy darkness
beneath the garden
earthworms absorb

bacilli through
their epithelia
while fine white threads

of mycelia reach
into the cells of the woody stalk
and hard husk of sunflower

nourishing the roots
of the elderberry
offering the fruit

we harvest and simmer down
to a thick syrup of darkness
we consume a spoon at a time

Dust

Sometimes I feel the presence
of the dead, only to convince myself later
it was merely a shadow moving on the far wall
of my desire to see beyond the curtain
between here and there as if loss
were merely a matter of waiting
in a room for the return of love, a chance
to undo or unsay, but no
amount of time will bring back those
we've lost because they never abandoned us.
We abandoned them by staying alive.

If I were to die my father said
preparing his will
and I wanted to say but didn't
there's no *if* about it.
The only certainty is that life doesn't last.
We have a string of moments and move on.

When my daughter stands in front of me,
a grown woman concerned about my health,
I remember the child and my hand on her forehead
feeling the fever, a necessary excess of will
spilling into the world, and I remember
her diving into the deep end of the pool
in a game of Gator, swimming along the bottom
well below the bigger boys who tried
to catch her, part of the game
continued even now.

And when my son lifts a giant wooden beam
over his head and holds it
while the other carpenters secure the ends,
the householder stands with her arms crossed,
eyes wide, momentarily awed
by the magnificent strength of this one man.

And everyone...my daughter caring for patients
in a small Botswana hospital,
my son rehabbing houses
after rehabbing himself,
their mother designing a playground
in unceded Mi'kmaq land,
the carpenters, the householder,
the woman laboring in a narrow bed,
even the child swinging high in the air
her shoes tied by love
and pointed toward heaven
will soon die and be forgotten.

And then it's dawn. Unexpected
light comes through the window
with graceful possibility.
The distinct nothingness of my life
suddenly seems glorious,
a particle of dust dancing in the light
beside eight billion others
while outside, a boy glides by on a bicycle
delivering the important stories of the day.

II.

The Trojan Women

There are moments when the elixir of
life rises to such overbrimming splendor
that the soul spills over.
　　　—Henry Miller, *Sexus*

Fortune's path is the reeling of a madman.
　　　—Euripides, *The Trojan Women*

The Trojan Women

Today in the Classic Cars website, I saw an ad for a fully
restored 1965 GMC pickup with a hard-shell camper hood, and
I thought of Henry and how he must have looked when he was
new, long before Julie and I made fumbling love in the bed in
back. I called, but the truck was already sold.

When I was 16, Dad paid $400 for a beater to haul gravel, dirt,
rosebushes and azaleas for his large garden in our backyard
where my brother Ken and I worked as indentured servants.
I remember being up to my knees in muck one afternoon and
seeing my gorgeous blonde sister Beth climb on the back of
a cool guy's Harley and roar off, and I wondered what exciting
adventures awaited her. I was older than Beth, but still naive in
a way she never was, and that afternoon I envied her because
she'd finished her chores and was free to have fun. Little did
any of us know that even then she was in serious trouble. In
those days, I thought that how I felt was the single most impor-
tant thing in life, and the possibility of dying was a fairy tale
invented by adults to scare children. Since Dad needed the pick-
up only on Saturday mornings, the rest of the week it became
my vehicle. I named it Henry, after Henry Miller whose *Tropic
of Cancer* held me in thrall.

Miller's bad boy narrator—a thief, a fornicator, an artist, and
a nihilist—had moved to Paris to be alone, ponder his despair
in seclusion, needing to walk through the sunshine and cobble-
stones of the Left Bank without companions or conversation,
face to face with himself, only the music of his heart for company.
Of course, this romantic notion of life seems like utter hogwash
to me now, fifty years later, but for a 16-year-old autistic boy
on the outskirts of Houston with no one to talk to except the
characters in books, the life of a brilliant vagabond living by
his wits in Paris sounded like heaven. Having no discernible
personality of my own, I adopted his. The Artist. Now all I had
to do was to find my medium. I tried painting but wasn't very
good at it. The poems I wrote didn't impress even my mother.

My music teacher hinted that I may be tone deaf. And when I
danced, I looked—as one cruel boy pointed out—like "a spastic
robot." Aspiring to be an artist when you have no obvious talent
is disheartening.

I finally found my niche backstage in school plays. *Technical
Director* was my title, but everybody called me Tech Guy. My ob-
session with learning obscure details and my tendency to stand
to the side and let others speak for me paid off, and I became
the one who made sure the perfect cone of amber light always
embraced the perfect form of Helen of Troy—aka Julie K. of my
math class and the prettiest girl in the whole damned school. I
began to pursue Helen/Julie with a persistence that only people
on the spectrum are capable of. I wooed her, finding my voice
as a poet, writing poems late at night (*the razzmatazz of her
toes*), memorized the poems, then when we were alone (*in the
ampersand of the moonlit dance*) I said the verse to her casually,
in conversation, as if I'd just thought of the lines.

It worked! She fell in love with me, and I was joyously, drunk-
enly, serenely in love with her. No longer like a book on a shelf
unread, my best impulses squelched, with her I became Henry
Miller, restless artist, wanderer who'd finally found the edge
of the world and jumped off. No longer a lost boy, no longer a
ridiculous lonely soul, I was now a man with a purpose: Tech
Guy bringing light to *The Trojan Women* by Euripides, the
greatest anti-war play ever written. Although, as our teacher ex-
plained, the play took only second prize at the Dionysian festival,
losing to a tragedy by Xenocles, an execrable poet. Aristophanes
mused at the time that the jury who chose Xenocles over Eurip-
ides had to have been either bribed or stupid. My adolescent
sense of justice fumed at the idea that Euripides, who now had
surpassed even Henry Miller himself as The Greatest Poet Who
Ever Lived, would be upstaged by a no-talent pretender who
fixed a contest twenty-four hundred years ago.

Euripides' play opens outside the fallen walls of the sacked city
where the noblewomen of Troy grieve their sons and husbands
and wait to be taken away as slaves. Queen Hecuba awakens in

shadows that I, Tech Guy, create, and she curses Helen as the cause of their misery. Menelaus, a weak officious man and the husband of Helen, enters stage left bathed in a sickly yellow light; with him is the Greek herald Talthybius, a decent sensitive man caught up in a world of depravity and grief, the only man in the play with any virtue. Menelaus pays him no heed, having come to Troy only to avenge his honor. Helen enters, pleading for her life, claiming she's the victim of a curse, but Hecuba scorns her excuse, as does Menelaus, and Helen is led off as a slave. At the end of the play, the bloody body of Hecuba's small grandson Astyanax is brought out on a shield, having been thrown from the castle walls by the Greeks who feared he'd seek revenge someday if allowed to live. With flames rising from the ruins of Troy, Hecuba makes a last attempt to kill herself but is restrained and taken with the other women to the ships of their captors.

Our high school rendition brought a standing ovation after every performance. Audiences roared with tears in their eyes. And I have to say, we deserved it—the performance was great. Patti J., the 17-year-old junior who played Hecuba, somehow found the despair of a ruined grandmother in her soul, and my lovely Julie played Helen as a woman who knew how to seduce men. Her Helen was perfectly balanced between vixen and gamine, evoking embarrassed desire in every man and suspicious rage in every woman. And I was proud of my work, especially the flickering flames of Troy on the back curtain, created by quickly passing red and yellow gels over the Fresnel lamp. Our play swept the local competitions leading to the state championship in Austin where we won, like Euripides, second place, losing to a faddish modernist piece no one reads anymore.

After high school, our troupe went our separate directions. Patti went to Yale and eventually became a successful playwright. My brother Ken inherited Henry and drove him hard until the driveshaft fell off. My sister Beth went to live with her cool Harley guy, hiding the arrangement from our parents. Julie and I went to different colleges and found other loves.

Two years later when I was visiting Houston during winter break, I had lunch with Julie, and she caught me up with the strange turns her life had taken since high school. She said she experienced a mental breakdown in college and spent time in a psychiatric hospital where she fell in love with one of the orderlies. When she was released, she went to live with him. He'd lost his job at the hospital after the affair with Julie was discovered, and they quickly became desperate for money, so he introduced her to a friend, a bellboy at a four-star hotel who turned her out to service the guests. She was sexy and beautiful and very popular with the male guests at the hotel, so she got top dollar for her efforts, but of course most of the money went to her two pimps. After a few months, she began to take stock of her life and felt ashamed of what she was doing. When she told her boyfriend she wanted to quit, he demanded she continue. They needed the money, he said. They argued and—here the details get a little murky—she shot him with his own pistol. The DA charged Julie with 2nd degree murder. At the trial she pleaded self-defense, and the jury acquitted her. As she told me this, I remembered how brilliantly she'd played Helen years before, and I wondered if she drew on that role as she testified on her own behalf in court.

At the time I talked with her, Julie was working for the law firm that had defended her, on her knees every day giving blow jobs to the attorneys to pay off her debt. I was twenty years old and wanted to be a hero, save her from the slave ship, so to speak, but of course I had no money and no power. I didn't dare ask my father for money to save my former girlfriend from prostitution. I carried the weight of my guilt, wondering about my role in her tragedy. As her first seducer, was I culpable? She and I parted, promising to stay in touch, but we didn't. A few months later, my mother ran into Julie downtown and, not knowing her story, encouraged me to call her. But after everything Julie had told me, I couldn't bear the thought of being with her. Selfishly, I blamed her for destroying my innocence, as if I were the victim, not her. Then, a year after our lunch, I heard from a mutual friend that Julie had told the head of the law firm to go to hell, threatened to report him to the bar, and moved to Colorado. My heart leapt with joy for her. At least one woman had escaped the slave ship.

It's been almost fifty years since I last saw Julie. Thinking of the long-ago past, as I often do these days, I recently searched for her on the internet. I found the obituary of her father, survived by his daughter Julie who had taken a different last name and now lived in a suburb of Dallas. Facebook led me to a picture of a beautiful young woman, a perfect ringer for my own Helen of Troy, standing in a backyard with two small children. She was exactly as I remembered Julie but a little older, perhaps early thirties. So, this beautiful young woman must be Julie's daughter, I realized, and these two children must be Julie's grandchildren. Then I saw a picture of an attractive older woman. Divorced and serene, she seemed genuinely happy. She was still beautiful—no longer Helen, but Hecuba. Her daughter and grandchildren spoke affectionately of her. I considered contacting her, but what would I say? Remember the good old days? I thought it best to let her enjoy her well-earned serenity without being reminded of what was probably the worst period of her life.

I hope Julie recovered from the horror and humiliation of what men did to her although I believe we can never completely shed our pasts. When I think of a beautiful girl enslaved to men and money, I think of my sister Beth who was trapped in the same way. She was forced into prostitution when she was still in high school, kidnapped, kept in a cage for days at a time, and gang-raped repeatedly. Twenty years later, she shot herself in a bathroom in Llano, Texas. On a bad day, the image I have of Julie and Beth is that of the Trojan women waiting to be loaded on the ships like livestock, and a great void opens in me and I feel I'm falling into the black space of guilt and self-loathing. Am I Menelaus, unaware of my entitlement and concerned only with empty honor? Or perhaps I'm Talthybius, the last good man standing helplessly on the shore shaking my head while my comrades take turns with the women? The slaves in the dark hold of the ship cannot climb out or go back to where things went wrong. There's no light, no voice of comfort, just chaos and darkness where they must find their own peace without the kindness of others.

As for me, I did make it to Paris. When I was 21, I wandered the cobblestone streets of the Left Bank, broke and alert, in perpetual expectancy, at last staying loyal to the lonely words, the spontaneous longing, the ecstatic moment Julie helped me find. And now, fifty years later, it's good to be just plain happy, and every now and then something beyond happiness, something like bliss in the golden light of the Seine.

III.

Daisy

After you died, I pulled a copy of *Gatsby*
from your shelf—torn, underlined, smudged
with marginalia—but still beautiful
in an unbound unglued sort of way.
You once said you knew Daisy
better than you knew yourself,
no boundary between two agitated girls
crafted of words, as if
she'd come to inhabit you
or you her, and no one, not even me,
the brother who tried to protect you,
could stop your slow extinguishment
and final gesture.

I remember taking you to a party
where young men who knew *Gatsby*
fell in love with you. One poet
you spent a week with on my couch,
stoned and passionate, hearing no doubt
his heart beating faster and faster
as Daisy's white face came up to his own.
He knew that when he kissed this girl,
and forever wed his unutterable visions
to her perishable breath, his mind
would never romp again like the mind of God.
He asked you to marry him and you said yes,
then no, then yes, then it was time to leave,
and for years he asked me about you
with tender curiosity
even after you died.
                        Another,
a handsome playwright known
as a talented seducer of actresses,
was so frightened by your frank invitation
to fuck, he ran
and never mentioned you again.

And the shy novelist who wrote
like an angel was so taken by your laughter
he couldn't speak but stood
in front of you with his mouth open
like a baby bird chirping for a worm.
Ashamed of his wordlessness
in the face of your beauty, he grew angry,
shook an apology out and turned away.
I thought him pathetic, but you knew
no amount of fire or freshness can challenge
what a man will store up in his ghostly heart.

You eventually married an electrician,
a rough-handed stubborn man who loved you more
than others had. He stayed with you
though you wrecked every car he ever owned.
He paid your bail and you bore him
two stalwart sons. Llano, Texas,
was nothing like Daisy's New York,
no large parties where a girl could keep
her privacy, no *blue gardens*
where *men and girls came and went like moths*
among the whisperings and the champagne and the stars.

No such thing in small town Texas
where men and girls come and go like flies
on their way to the rodeo. Eventually
all the women gossiped
you'd been sold to men
and didn't care you'd been forced,
beaten and raped again and again,
finally escaping, not telling anyone,
even me, for twenty years.

How were you like Daisy,
a spoiled girl in love with luxury?
You were not spoiled, but ruined
by the brutality of men.
Perhaps it was Jay Gatsby's love

for Daisy you recognized,
how Howard would do anything
for you, build a house,
forgive again and again
your manic mistakes, your headlong
falls into disaster. Perhaps
like Daisy you were *a careless person,*
smashing up things and creatures
and then retreating to the care of your enablers
and their own *vast carelessness.*

And your poor husband. He'd come a long way
to this brown lawn on the far edge of Austin
and his dream must have seemed so close
that he could hardly fail to grasp it.
He did not know that it was already behind him,
somewhere back in that vast obscurity beyond the city,
where the dark fields of the republic rolled on under the night.

It was different for you. At times you felt it coming,
a haunting loneliness, and sensed it in others,
the young clerk in the tollbooth at dusk,
the waitress working the night shift at the roadside café,
wasting the most poignant moments of night and life....
as we drove on toward death through the cooling twilight.

Everyone Knows Death (I laughed at your funeral)

I loved you but your death seemed
Like a joke you were playing on us
People looked at me like I was crazy
And I suppose I was
The long faces the tears welling
The big casket for a small body
The women who were cruel to you
The men who desired you
The preacher who disapproved of you
The aunts who shook their heads at you
The boss who fired you
The policeman who arrested you
The psychologist who gave you pills
The father who blamed you
The sons who loved you
The husband who locked himself
In the bedroom for three days
The mother who said you were doing
So much better and now this
And me the brother you said
Could always make you laugh
Humor cut the pain in half
You said again at your funeral
As you sat beside me
In the seventh pew on the right side
Of nothing rolling your eyes
At the biddies and the bubbas
Speaking softly of the girl
Who blew her brains out
I thought if there's ever a time
When a good laugh is called for
This is it

The Pecan Grove

Shadow of the pecan tree sways
on the rusty screen. Cracked
porcelain of the kitchen

sink shines. The Irish Cherokee
girl shells pecans
until her fingers bleed, a bead

of sweat lingers on the ball
of her nose, hesitates and falls
on the flattened dough of pie crust

She is the salt that seasons, the soda
that leavens, the rolling pin that pushed
me into place. I imagine her in heaven

making pies—cherry chocolate peach pecan
mincemeat lemon (leave the seeds in
so they'll know it's real)

Pastries swollen like moons orbiting the holiday
Grandmother of my sorrow, grandmother
of my anger

        grandmother
of the hickory switch, fig tree
peach tree, cigarettes and coffee

the station wagon is leaving the driveway
a last time, children piled high
on blankets, a long sleep home

    *

Never a chance to say goodbye
to say how much I loved that boy
who was my grandfather

Mr. Cook his wife called him
as if he was all growed up
his daughters despised him

He taught me to crack
two pecans in a bare hand
spit and cuss like a man
cheat at solitaire

Gallivantin' around town
wasting money with his buddies
he taught me

the geometry of carpentry
the mysteries
of plumbing, told me
dirty jokes

He spent his daughters' college fund
on country club dues
so his daughters refused
to say a prayer over his body

Those four tight-lipped matrons
shipped off his body
a humanitarian donation

They put him on a stainless-steel table
sliced him from the hollow
of his throat
to the swell of his groin

They pulled out heart
liver, spleen
like you'd dump a bag
of groceries

I didn't see it
I wasn't there
I wasn't anywhere near
Texas Baylor Medical School

I was in Pittsburgh
Where my wife was making a wreath
of rowan and hemlock and dahlias

We went to the Point
where two rivers merge
and flow into another life

We threw the wreath
in the waters
and my small son
said *goodbye Daddy Cook*

and we watched the wreath
caught in two currents
floating, not moving

not moving at all
we went home
to our good life

Zelphia Irene Slavens Cook (1904–1983)
Melvin Arlin Cook (1905–1992)

Jesus

Sixteen and running
From my father's fists
I once tried to jump on a moving train

The way it happened was
It was the outskirts
Of evening

Outside Houston and a guy
Who said his name
Was Jesus

Came out of the cane fields
And started walking beside me
Which scared me

A little because he looked hungry
Not mean just
Hungry but I'd read my Steinbeck

And knew the code of the rails
No man can deny another man
The right to move

Which would've been fine
If I'd been a man instead
Of a scared boy

Who didn't know
He didn't know and here was
A real hobo

Named Jesus who asked me
Where I was going which was
Nowhere so I said

North sounding like I meant it
And asked where he
Was going

No perticlar place he said
And shrugged
And asked

Where I was from which was
Somewhere so I pointed
My chin South

And said *Bout seven mile that way*
Because that's how real hobos
Talk and he looked South

And said sadly *If I lived that close
I'd go home* and I knew
I'd never feel sadness

The way a real hobo feels sadness
And then we heard
A train coming

Behind us and we moved over
And waited and started running
And when the freight cars

Came by Jesus
Grabbed the ladder on the back
Of a car and swung

Himself up and I missed
And fell
In the gravel and

Lay there
Watching the caboose grow smaller
And smaller in the twilight

Delinquents

Cruising Houston
in a truck with my cousin
who had my name
but was a thug
Colonel Chicken
Mac 'n Fries
Paco Taco—
he named the city
as we lived it

petty thieves we
shoplifted candy
cigarettes cassettes
blasting *Can't Get No*
out the window

Michael G. had
a baseball bat
in the back seat
just in case
he said

we were rebels because
our families hated us
and our families
hated us because
we were rebels

we drank at a party
of thieves
celebrating Long John's
lucky run of 30 scores
in a month

Flash the Purse Snatcher
Sam the Tool who was good

at hotwiring
Pattycakes who worked
businessmen at

the Hilton and her
boyfriend Ricky Blades
and their small son
Bubba who later was shot

while robbing a gas station
with a toy gun
Greaser
who sold prescription pads

Beano who stole
purses from old ladies
and Blind Monkey
who wasn't blind
but played the long con

we partied until
we passed out and
years later I found out
Michael had raped

a 12-year-old kid
beating the boy
until he submitted
and scaring him so he

wouldn't tell
until long after Michael died
young
eaten by cancer

Raccoon

I used to see his eyes
shining in the dark
as he watched me
sitting on the kitchen
floor drinking my wife
had left taking
my last illusion
of a normal life the
raccoon who lived
in the bamboo thicket
of the bayou behind
our house visited me
in the dark every
morning I was a scared
little boy in a man's life
it was summer in Denton Texas
and the bug zapper made
a harsh rhythm electrocuting
mosquitoes in a way
I envied drinking myself
to death was taking
far too long the raccoon
would crawl through
the hole he'd torn
in the backdoor screen
pad casually across
the kitchen past me
help himself to
the cat food I think
he thought I was dead
or dying and by Jesus
he was right maybe
smelling of bourbon
and self-pity I was
his spirit animal or
maybe he just thought

I was a lump of rags
he needn't fear the cat
stayed away from him
hissing in the dark
living room sometimes
I forgot to fill the bowl
the raccoon would
sniff around the kitchen
filling his mouth with
stale kibble carry it
into the bathroom
dip the kibble in
the toilet eat it
Cassandra and that
was her actual name
had said either I get help
or go ahead and die
because she was tired
of waiting to see which
it would be to be fair
I couldn't decide so
how could she know
on the other side
of the bamboo where
the raccoon lived there
was a bar where students
drank I considered them
baby drunks and never
went there one early
morning the raccoon
and I were looking at
each other when
a car came crashing
through the bamboo
jumped the bayou
knocked down my
back fence the raccoon
ran like hell and I

went outside to find out
what happened there
was a young woman
drunk gunning the engine
her wheels spinning
in the air over the bayou
I offered to help
placed a few boards
from the fence under
the tires for traction
so she was able to
drive forward through
my backyard to my driveway
sped to the street and
disappeared and
I was standing there
completely baffled by
what just happened when
a young man came running
into my backyard with
a cop chasing him they
ran over my flattened fence
and into the parking lot
of the bar neither one
noticing me I went inside
for the first time
in days sat in a chair
and started laughing
uncontrollably at
the complete absurdity
of my life the next day
I stumbled into a meeting
where people I didn't know
knew me and knew
what lay before me
and eventually I stopped
drinking and began to heal
now decades later I live
in a different city with

a different wife different
life different fence and
tonight I'm up late
because I'm old and
the pills I take keep me
awake and I hear
a raccoon opening
our garbage cans and
Josie our plucky Kelpie
leaps off the porch and
attacks the raccoon who
turns and runs and
I feel free

Lunatic Lullaby (My son and I descend into love and madness together)

Many fears ago
When my son was broken
He somehow found the strength to walk the long mountain
To our house and collapse into my arms
And I somehow found the strength to carry him
As I did when he was a baby
Hold his unstill head
Give him a sip of water and croon him a song

He was seeing demons, just as I have
And I rocked him to sleep

At 5 a.m. my wife calls
On her drive to work
She sees our son
Standing barefoot on a street corner
Singing softly
To himself

Is he singing the song I hear
When I'm mad?

Let me lull you my lullaby
Sweet lunatic
With the lunatic lullaby
The strange ballad
Sung by the loneliest of all
The lowly lunatic

Does my son wake
As I have
Unable to breathe
A great darkness opening
In front of him?

Does music emerge
From the walls?
Do words call
From the dark?

Does he fly low
Over the water
Stars on the flecked waves
A fin, a wing, a prow
And the far shore rises
A forest where eyes
Are staring out?

Does he hear this song?

Let this lullaby
Of the lunatic
The lunatic's lullaby
Enter your heart
Calling the dark

Don't fear the lullaby
My lunatic
The lunatic's lullaby
The melody can't hurt
If you're already mad

Oh my sweet harm
Drink the tears
Before I sleep
I hope to die
Before I cry
Cry, cry, crime

Do the voices tell him
It's so much better when you die?
They're gone, they're gone
It's better when you're dead

All those things left unsaid
They're gone, they're gone

While you sobbed my name
Again and again the same
For you I sing this lullaby
I'll try
Again I'll try

I spit the truth you made me swallow
I push the soil you pulled me under
I need you buried
Deeply buried

(When a boy hides his pain
The man lives in shame)

Happy dog. Happy happy dog. Happy dog.

Sacred Sleep

My father often woke me
in the dark hours
to discuss minor sins
I'd committed.
If I weren't alert enough
to say what he wanted to hear
he'd strike me without warning
and walk away satisfied
with the discipline he enforced
in his prescription-induced rage.

So now my sleep is punctuated with terror
and excursions into weirdness
and I sleep with one eye open
like a prey animal peering into darkness.
For Eva, who had loving parents,
sleep is not a descent into madness
but a flight on the back of a great bird
headed for a distant valley
where serenity can always be found.

Oh to dream like Merlin
sleeping forever in a magical forest
where his beautiful enchantress visits
every evening. But no, my sleep's the version
where the Lady of the Lake throws Merlin in a pit
and the Great Mage is never heard from again.
No death's dream for him,
only long oblivion in the dark
while night-worms crawl on his flesh.

I remember as a boy escaping
to the stables on a summer night.
The moon shone down on the metal gate.
Puppies lay in a furry mound,
wrapped around each other

in a thick disk of contentment
while big dogs rested nearby.
Horses stood in their stalls sleeping,
later lying down, settling into straw
to dream of whatever horses dream of
when they're protected and well-fed.

Some whales can go a month
without sleeping. Drifting
on the waves with their pods,
they take turns descending into slumber,
pups dozing beside their mothers.
Cuvier's beaked whales can dive
10,000 feet into utter darkness
and sleep for hours at a time
without breathing.

Lying in the darkness with my wife
I'm thinking of the infinite space
between waking and sleeping,
how Black Elk traveled far from his body
in a pure quest to save his people.
He knew only in sleep are we fully aware,
only in sleep can we let go of what we think
we know is real, let the sharp edges fall away,
only in sleep can we embrace our true selves.

If I surrender to loving
this woman with my whole being
and let nothing else touch my heart
then whoever I may be
or whatever I do or try to do
my love will never be extinguished
and I will find its likeness in all things
and I will no longer seek peace
because it is already mine.

Sometimes I Wake Early

Sometimes I wake early and walk through the house
touching doors that swing into darkness
my bare toes searching out
toys and magazines

Outside it might be raining, a full wind
filling the trees like sails. I sit
in the love seat under the bay window, hugging
myself, letting the children's dreams wash over me
like waves

Last night we took a friend for a walk along the edge
of our mountain. She looked out
over the city, the rivers, the sultry slopes
crowded with sumac and maple
and said *So you know where you live*

Yes, in the darkness and rain
our small house stands in a huddle of houses
under the clouds, in a story
we ourselves are telling

Inventory

Waking from our 11,386th night together
After 7 automobiles, 6 refrigerators, 4 washer/dryers
3 stoves, 3 furnaces, 2 houses in 1 neighborhood
9 jobs, mostly mine
7 published books
4 nonprofit corporations
2 for-profit businesses
And of course 2 dogs
and 2 children

Uncountable fevers and injuries
Tensions and arguments

Griefs and joys

I just want to say
We couldn't have done it
Without us

And also I want to say
By the way, not so incidentally
As we're finishing our 22,772nd pot of coffee
And you get dressed to work in the garden
Which now at the end of the season
Still has roughly 50 roses and 100 zinnias
And a volunteer squash vine
Which is climbing over the hedge
And bothering the neighbor,
You still look pretty damn good
In a pair of jeans

Puppy Rolling

A poet asked me to write a blurb for the back cover of his new book.
I said yes and wrote a few nice things about his poems. He wrote
back saying he'd tweaked my blurb and sent the new version. Man,
it was nothing like what I'd written. But the thing is, it made me
look really smart, like I completely understood the inner workings
and meanings of his poetry, almost as if I were living in the poet's
mind when he was writing the darn things, as if I'd stayed up late
with him discussing whether *fresh as a daisy* is, well, fresh enough
for a poem, so I said yes, go ahead, use the blurb you wrote, it's
much better than mine because the way I see it, writing blurbs
is kind of like puppy rolling. *Say what,* you say. It's like this: When
I take Josie to the dog park she likes to find a puppy, preferably
a rare breed like a Shiba Inu or a New Guinea Singing Dog and
roll it down the hill. It doesn't hurt the puppies. In fact, they seem
to enjoy being rolled, but sometimes the owner, usually somebody
who's never accidentally dropped a baby or stuck a baby with
a safety pin or taken eyes off the kid for five seconds and had to
run into traffic to save it, somebody who thinks puppies are fragile,
gets upset and tells me to stop rolling her puppy which I can't
really do, my dog having a mind of her own, so we just have to
leave the park. All of this explains why when the poetry critic posted
a comment saying he disagreed with the blurb I didn't actually
write what could I say—it wasn't my dog? Instead, I just said
I understood his concern over the fragility of American poetry, it
being a rare breed and all, and unfriended him.

Names

Lea wants to change her name to Tina.
Her mother says she must think very carefully
      because a name has to fit.
The wrong name can bind like someone else's shoes.
Who knows where a name has walked,
dust of what roads, uncomfortable creases across the toes,
the heel worn down by someone else's sorrow?

Her brother says the name Tina fits.
But if she's Tina, what happened to Lea?
The name turned down the wrong street, got lost,
fell off the edge of the mountain.
The sound of her name fills the river valley.
Everywhere it is nowhere, he says,
her name needs to come home.

Lea doesn't want to be Tina anymore.
It's just too much responsibility.

The Happiness of Animals

When the soul-sickness takes me
And my mind is in an ugly place
And I resent other writers their success, I retire to my attic room
To look out the small window at the gray street dead leaves carried by
    the wind I hear a storm coming

And I am no longer the ruler of my invisible kingdom
And incomparable ecstasy is no longer at my beckoning
And the honey of praise for my children is no longer on my lips
And I am not the man I planned to be nor is this the life I wanted
And my feet have forgotten the music and my hands have forgotten
    the smooth arcs
And the gift I once had is a black wand that goads me into self-loathing
And the small cruelties I've practiced seem large and the large irreparable
And even the innocence of William Blake cannot console me
My son says he's cracked the code

*Dad, when you put your head under the pillow you're dreaming deeply and
    don't bother you*
*And when you lie in bed staring at the ceiling you're working on a poem and
    don't bother you*
*And when you lie on your back with your arms across your face then we
    especially better not bother you*

Then I hear bees and ghosts of bees swarming.
And I worry that I've become like Maureen the Madwoman
    of Mount Washington
Pursued by penguins and weasels through the streets
Screaming her shrill mantra *Spider web spider web*
Let down your hair repeated all day all night
Until Ed Shaw the beat cop tells her to move on move on

I pull the shades
I lie down in the dark and listen to the rain
I hear my daughter sitting on the carpet with crayons saying
The heart is two circles and a dot

The heart is two circles and a dot
And I remember Robert Herrick speaking of his lady's *spicy nest*
The scent of my wife moving from room to room
I begin to believe the curve is the holiest of inventions
And my daughter asks *Dad, how come all your friends are in AA or else
    some kind of animal?*
And I listen to the *Goldberg Variations* until I swear I will never write
    another poem about an angel dragging a broken wing
From now on I will praise only the beauty of logarithms, how they are like
    elegant jewels on a golden chain
And I sing off-key until I realize I've almost figured out the equation of joy
And I write down everything the madwoman says, turning each line this
    way and that
And I call to my dog Winchester—we walk the forgotten streets in the last
    of the warm rain
We wade in the waist-high weeds of an abandoned lot
Where Winchester, a black lion in a peaceable kingdom,
Grazes on the daffodil and azalea and asphodel,
And I consider the dirt under my shoe, how old it is
Older than arithmetic, older than spoons and mirrors and scissors
Perhaps as old as the happiness of animals
The happiness of a cow lying in a meadow chewing her memory
Of sunlight and grass
Chewing everything twice
Coughing it up, spitting it out
Like a poet

House

You want to lie down in the lost field
of your courage and sleep
beside the blurred road of snow

But a lamp is waiting in the window
The house looks out through the keyhole
it is warm
children sleeping in their nests

Here in the heart of the circle
a woman playing guitar
turns you inside out
like a glove

Here is like a dark summer

Outside the night is smooth black water
the entire universe
a constellation of houses in the hills

You among those
who have built
stone on stone
a house in the wind

IV.

Death and the Maiden

I used to tease my friend Gil he was a dead
ringer for the young Schubert
when he was composing the *Lieder*

we loved when we were young
lifted by their spare lines
and delicate colors, the marriage

of music and verse, the rush
of feeling, the sharp pain
of beauty that catches your breath.

But now we're old enough to enjoy
the Schubert of *Death and the Maiden*,
his masterpiece which began as a song

and slowly grew into a dark terror
after he realized he was dying
from syphilis. In terrible pain,

penniless and despairing, he wrote
to a friend that love and friendship
had become torture, and even

his enthusiasm for the beautiful
had vanished. In *Death and the Maiden*
he's a man looking into darkness and singing.

Thinking he'd accomplished his greatest work,
he asked his friend the famous violinist
Ignaz Schuppanzigh to lead the quartet.

The old maestro, who by this time was so fat
he could barely play in tune, pretended
to be unimpressed. *Brother, this is nothing at all,*

let well enough alone: stick to your Lieder.
Schubert was crushed and put the sheets away
They weren't published until three years after his death.

*

*And what, my friend Gil asks, did I do
that warrants this punishment
of guilt and worry? I once pulled*

*the car over and told Maria
we wouldn't leave until she kissed me.
So she kissed me. Was that so awful?*

*We lay down in the grass
and I taught her the stars
but never touched her*

*I swear. And now she's writing
letters condemning me.
Other women are stepping forward*

*to accuse me as well, but it was only
Maria I loved. She was my muse,
my inspiration. With her I felt young.*

Maria writes: *He was sixty. I was sixteen.
He was my teacher and I trusted him.
No man should behave this way.*

*

Schubert's quartet takes its name
from the poem by Matthias Claudius
which appears in the second movement

where the Maiden protests while Death
seduces her with terror and comfort.
The Maiden cries *Oh! leave me!*

Prithee, leave me! thou grisly man
Of bone! For life is sweet, is pleasant.
Go! leave me now alone! Go!

Leave me now alone!
And Death responds:
Give me thy hand,

Oh! maiden fair to see, for I'm a friend,
Hath ne'er distress'd thee.
Take courage now, and very soon

Within mine arms shalt softly rest thee!
The composition races
through pain, terror, resignation

and ends with a tarantella
to ward off madness, the endless
dance of pitiless desire.

Nightjar

Why should I care
whether automobiles carry dead drivers
off the empty highway into the forest?

Should it bother me
if influential briefcases
no longer swing
through the canyons?

Or empty suits forget
how to climb the stone stairs
of the courthouse? Should I feel sad
when the giant steel cages
hold only the bones of men?

I'd love to watch
skyscrapers collapse from within,
each floor heavy with the years,
windows widening to let the wind
blow the important pages away
like so many lies.

Shouldn't we rejoice
when great ocean liners no longer
plow the plastic sea to unhappy islands
but lie in the coral dark, mollusks
building calcium palaces on their hulls?

God who once loved us
no longer requires our praise,
delighting Himself alone
with the meadowlark.

A crow lifts an unseemly voice to heaven,
and a nightjar flies over the ruined houses
carrying a soul, passing it
from one bird to the next,
never content with its song.

The Ruins

Imagine
the tall blue heron
wading at the edge,
rings of water extending
from impossibly thin legs,

the air full
of transparent wings,

the fox crossing
the innocent road
full of weeds.

Picture the ruins of the house
where coyotes now raise their young,
and bears have returned
to search for honey.

Think of mice
carving nests in the books
of the library, and otters
sliding down the banks
of the river behind
the crumbling Exxon,

bees nesting in the eaves
of the mayor's old mansion
and termites chewing through
the pile of newspapers
in the attic.

No one misses us,
not even the dog
who loved us
and praised us
as we praise God.

What It Wasn't

It wasn't bigger than a breadbox.
It wasn't smooth as glass.
It didn't smell good or bad
Or have any taste whatsoever.

It didn't make a sound.
It didn't offend or flatter.
It wasn't what you might call
Well-mannered in the least.

It didn't ask any questions
Or have any answers.
It didn't raise any issues
Except maybe one.

What could we do
But put it in a lonely spot,
Light the fuse, cover our brains
And run?

The Real Deal

Last night I dreamed I saw
Charles Bukowski on the street
slapping his wife Linda Lee around
while strangers watched and cheered
laughing and saying *He's the Real Deal*
and Linda Lee looking me in the eye
and silently mouthing *Please*
which I thought was a beckoning
so as the Real Deal lifted
his hand to strike her again
I grabbed his arm and the crowd grew
hostile so I stared them down
tied Buk's arms behind him with
a piece of rope I conveniently had
threw him in the trunk of my car
and drove him to an AA meeting
where he sat swaying drunkenly
as a man who'd just been released
from prison spoke about forgiving
the gangster who killed his son and
someone I sponsored talked about
burning his house down
killing his father because
Jesus told him to and
a woman spoke of wiping out
an entire family on the highway
but Buk wasn't listening
instead looking at the door
trying to wriggle free of the ropes
wanting to go back to his life
of chaos and cruelty
and finally when it was his turn
to speak he called us all
pussies tore free from his
bonds ran to the window
and leaped growing black wings

in midflight circling the neighborhood
twice and landing on the sidewalk
in front of a bar where Linda Lee
was waiting for him and Buk dropped
his wings and he and Linda Lee walked
into the bar hand in hand so I guess
Linda Lee liked being married
to the Real Deal even if it meant
a black eye now and then and
she liked people applauding
the Real Deal who had a talent
for bravado and I woke thinking
I can't blame them for loving him
because Buk speaks to our need
to tear free from acceptable
over-revised poems I read
in journals which act
like well-behaved teenagers
showing up at the front door
dressed for the prom and wanting
their pictures taken while I like a poem
showing up at the back door
needing a haircut shirt untucked
and mud on its boots from a long
hike through the woods and fields
and alleys and perhaps a fossil
hanging onto the tongue
of the boot which the poem
notices for the first time when
I point it out and offers the crusty
bone to me since I love old things
in new packages especially
if they have a little dirt on them

The Great Conjunction

December 21, 2020

It's the night of the Great Conjunction,
Jupiter and Saturn merging in the sky
forming the Christmas Star, and also
it's the Winter Solstice.

I think of Wise Men
following their star, and
our ancestors building bonfires
to tempt the sun to warm the fields.
I think of the sun rising between
great standing stones,
and the Persians gathering for Yaldā Night
to eat pomegranates
and recite the poems of Hafiz.

In America,
we've been in quarantine
six months, seeing almost no one
as the days darken.
It's the birthday of my sister,
my beautiful sister Elizabeth
who killed herself thirteen years ago.

A conjunction of darknesses...
the night lit by a single star
which isn't a star at all
but two giant globes of ice—
they'll have to do.

Great Jupiter, King of Cosmic Law,
Saturn, Bringer of Prosperity,
where are You now
in our godless country
ruled by liars and thieves
cheered by a chorus of fools?

Flood and Fire

"The statistical analysis of proximate and ultimate features of the
sequential collapse reveals the relationships of climate-driven famine,
sea-borne invasion, region-wide warfare, and politico-economic collapse,
in whose wake new societies and new ideologies were created."
— *David Kaniewski, et al. "Environmental Roots of the Late Bronze Age Crisis"*

I write these words for you
who will come later, after
we're gone. The destruction

I imagine will be complete.
Even now the western fires
are spreading

from forests to towns
and the skies are red at night
and black at dawn. The sea

is rising. The sky is roiling.
The airports are filled
with abandoned passengers.

Our southern
border is besieged
by families running from wars

we started and we hear
of boats crowded
with children

sinking under the waves
and thousands of people shot
by police. Mobs swirl

in the streets but
tear gas batons and bullets
cannot stop the rising calls

for justice. Last week a Nazi
driving into a surging crowd
was pulled from his car

and beaten. Our leaders
implore us to be calm, others
urge us to resist and still others

tell us to hate. Even now
when a plague is upon us
taking our very breath away

many still deny
our time has passed, claiming
only the old are dying.

Yesterday I stepped over
a homeless woman,
Mother Mary of the Sidewalk

someone called her,
and I turned my eyes away
incapable of shame.

It's too late to save any of us.
So I say to you
who come later, after

the cities are smoking
ruins, piles of brick
and ash,

large ships have nowhere
to sail to and
small ships have sunk

in the harbors—
I say to you please learn
from our mistakes.

We didn't listen to those
who came before,
the Old Ones who told us

the earth is our Mother,
the sky our Father.
We are Their children

but we did not honor them.
We stripped the land
of its minerals, leaving only

poisons flowing into streams.
We killed the aborigines
who lived close to the earth.

We took everything
for ourselves, never
thinking of you

and for this we should not be
forgiven. Judge us harshly.
Our sins were many.

We invented terrible weapons
and profited from war.
We were cruel to those

who trusted us, putting children
in cages to punish
their parents, locking

animals in vast warehouses,
their waste seeping into
lakes and streams.

The animals lived
under the florescence
of our craving, never

able to see sunlight, and now
in an odd turn
of justice, wild pigs destroy

our crops and groves
and coydogs thrive
in our cities, growing larger

and bolder, eating
our pets and someday
our children. And I

who thought myself
a just man,
educated and prosperous,

quick to give
a beggar a dollar,
I who laughed at the idea

of God, the solace of
the ignorant, now
sit on my roof,

the street below
a dangerous river, scribbling this
missive you will never read,

waiting for unlikely help
from above, and in
desperation ask Him

or Her or It
to save us from what we ourselves
created.

Envoi

Oh poor dear
Broken America

To whom will you
Leave your bars
And laundromats?
Who will inherit
The warehouses
Of the dying?
Who will want
The poisoned soil
The Gideon Bibles
The libraries of ghosts?

The Turn

An old woman is swimming laps
At the Y, graceful and fast—
I time her at 30 seconds a lap

36 minutes a mile
Almost twice my speed. Of course
I'm a plodder, no Mark Spitz

But still I'm impressed
By the efficiency of her strokes.
She overhands on her back

Until 8 feet from the wall, she
Flips on her stomach, crawls 2 strokes
Dives, spins and pushes gently

Off the wall in a perfect turn.
How long has she practiced
These succinct movements
So free of affectation?

        And so unlike
Isadora moving as if made of wind,
A creature of pure invention,

Pure expression, she thrived on attention.
Zelda wrote how she and Scott sat
In a Paris café, watching a drunk

Duncan. He later spoke
Of how memorable she was
But what Zelda recalled

Was that while all eyes
Were watching Duncan,
Zelda was able to steal

The salt and pepper shakers
From the table.

        Isadora died at 50,
A victim of her own need
To perform her beauty.
On a September night

In Nice, a passenger in a car
Owned by Benoît Falchetto,
A gorgeous Italian mechanic,

Isadora wore a long flowing
Hand-painted silk scarf
Created by the Russian

Artist Roman Chatov, a gift
From her friend Mary Desti,
The mother of Preston Sturges,

Stars all. Desti suggested Isadora
Wear a cape in the open-air vehicle
Because it was a cold night

But Isadora wanted the enormous
Scarf to blow behind her,
An exquisite banner. As they departed

She said to Desti *"Je vais à l'amour"*
Meaning she and Falchetto
Were off to her hotel for a tryst.

The draped scarf around her neck
Wafting behind her as she stood
With the wind in her face

Became entangled in the spoke
Of a wheel, hurling her
From the car to the stone

Pavement, killing her instantly,
Leading to Gertrude Stein's
Famous mordant remark

Affectations can be dangerous.
Good advice. Isadora's pose
Killed her which

Leads me to wonder
If Isadora had lived
Another 30 years,

Would she have lost
Her affectation? If we live
Long enough do we lose

Our craving for *tableau
vivant*? Does our art strip down
To the smallest gesture?

   And so
It's the old dancers that fascinate me.
Training every day as the body resists,
The spirit lifts them into clarity.

*Everything happens at 100,
Everything changes,* Eileen Kramer
Says. Her life, she says,

Has become magical and she dances
With soft sinuous gestures
That move like billowing folds
Of fabric.

   Men too
sometimes flower in our last years.
I think of Yeats in his 70s

Casting a cold eye
On Ben Bulben, his grave
In a windy churchyard far

From the snow-white girls posing
In the salley gardens
Of his youth. And I think

Of the practical and visionary
Mandela, having so impressed
The warder that he spent

His last few years in prison
As a guest in the warder's home.
By then, all pretension had been seared

From him by the years of study
And meditation in confinement.
Leaving prison, Mandela

Held Winnie's hand
In front of a huge crowd, the event
Broadcast across the world.

He gave a speech pledging
Peace and reconciliation
And thus began a new era.

As for me, my accomplishments
Are meager in comparison
But I did teach myself to swim

At the age of 36. By the end
Of the summer I swam a mile
Every day and beside me

My mentor Mel, 40 years older,
Swam 2 miles a day, then went home,
Ate a tuna sandwich, watched *Sesame Street*

And came back to the gym
To play basketball. I asked him once
Why *Sesame Street*? And he responded

Joy is the source
Of wisdom, something I've pondered
Every day since.

Notes

Most of the poems in this collection were written during the Covid pandemic, January 2020 to April 2021; but a few of the poems were written in 1997 when my children Nicholas and Lea were young.

Nigel: The italicized lines of the poem are direct quotations from an article in *The Telegraph*, 2 February 2018: "Nigel the Lonely Gannet dies on island surrounded by concrete birds" by Mike Malloy.

Compost: See http://compost.css.cornell.edu/invertebrates.html for source information.

Daisy: An elegy for my sister Elizabeth Yeary. The italicized portions are quotations from *The Great Gatsby* by F. Scott Fitzgerald, my sister's favorite book.

The phrase *Lunatic Lullaby* is borrowed from the title of an anonymous nonsense song we sang around the campfire when I was a child:
Oh I was born at night one morn when the whistle went boom boom
You can buy a cake or fry a snake when the mud pies are in bloom
Does six and six make nine? Does ice grow on a vine? etc.

Nightjar refers to a large family of nocturnal insect-eating birds sometimes called *nighthawks*. The name *nightjar* reflects the European folk-belief that the birds suckle goats by night, causing them to cease giving milk. The American whip-poor-will, a species of nightjar, is said to have the ability to sense a soul departing and can capture it as it flees.

Death and the Maiden: The tarantella is a dance, believed by scholars to be descended from a Dionysiac cult, in which the dancer and the drum player constantly try to upstage each other by playing faster or dancing longer than the other.

Flood and Fire: See Kaniewski D, Van Campo E, Guiot J, Le Burel S, Otto T, Baeteman C (2013) *Environmental Roots of the Late Bronze Age Crisis.* PLoS ONE 8(8): e71004. https://doi.org/10.1371/journal.pone.0071004

Acknowledgments

The author is grateful to the editors of the following journals where many of these poems, often in earlier versions, were published:

5AM, The Banyan Review, Black Warrior Review, Cultural Weekly, DoveTales, MiGozine, The Non-Conformist, The Pittsburgh Quarterly, Pittsburgh Post-Gazette, Plant-Human Quarterly, PoetryMagazine.com, Sampsonia Way, Texas Observer, Uppagus, Writers at Large and *Writing for Peace.*

Some of these poems were read by the author on Jan Beatty's radio show *Prosody* aired by WYEP Pittsburgh, others by the author on *The Karen Denard Show* aired by KERA Dallas, and still others by Lauren Camp on *Audio Saucepan* aired by KSFR Santa Fe.

Some of these poems appeared in two chapbooks by Michael Simms: *The Happiness of Animals* and *Black Stone* published by Ziggy Edwards under the imprint Monkey Sea Editions.

Some of these poems were published in *The Fire-eater,* a chapbook by Michael Simms, published by Del Marie Rogers.

Many of these pieces were included in the blog *Note from the Editor* published by Vox Populi.

* * *

I'd like to thank the staff of Ragged Sky Press—Ellen Foos, publisher; Arlene Weiner, editor; and Jean Foos, designer—for their impressive professionalism that made this book possible.

I'd also like to thank Naomi Shihab Nye and Don Wentworth for their generous praise and encouragement.

Most of all, I'm grateful to my wife Eva-Maria Simms whose love, patience and friendship have saved my life and made my life worth living. In addition, Eva's keen editorial eye and perfect pitch for the music of language had an incalculable influence on these poems.

Born and raised in Texas, **Michael Simms** has been active in politics and poetry for over 40 years as a writer, teacher, editor, and community activist. He is the founder of *Vox Populi*, an online forum for poetry, politics, and nature, as well as Autumn House Press, a nonprofit publisher of books of poetry, fiction, and nonfiction. He's also the author of three full-length collections of poetry and two college textbooks about poetry—and the lead editor of over 100 published books. Simms has won a number of awards and fellowships, including a Certificate of Recognition in 2011 from the Pennsylvania State Legislature for his contribution to the arts. Simms has an MFA from the University of Iowa and a Certificate in Plant-based Nutrition from Cornell University. He lives with his wife Eva in the historic Mount Washington neighborhood overlooking the city of Pittsburgh.